Saving the Peregrine Falcon

by Caroline Arnold / photographs by Richard R. Hewett

A Carolrhoda Nature Watch Book

Carolrhoda Books, Inc./Minneapolis

The photographs on the following pages are used through the courtesy of the Peregrine Fund: top of 15, 38, 40-41.
The photographs on the following pages are used through the courtesy of J. Jennings: 36, 42.
The author and photographer wish to express their appreciation.

Words that appear in **boldface** *in the text are defined in the glossary on page 48.*

This edition of this book is available in two bindings:
Library binding by Carolrhoda Books, Inc.
Soft cover by First Avenue Editions
c / o The Lerner Group
241 First Avenue North
Minneapolis, Minnesota 55401

LIBRARY OF CONGRESS CATALOGING IN PUBLICATION DATA

Arnold, Caroline.
    Saving the peregrine falcon.

    "A Carolrhoda nature watch book."
    Includes glossary.
    Summary: Describes the efforts of scientists who are trying to save the Peregrine falcon from extinction by taking the fragile eggs that would not survive in the wild, hatching them, raising the chicks, and then releasing the birds back into the wild.
    1. Peregrine falcon—Juvenile literature. 2. Birds, Protection of—Juvenile literature. [1. Peregrine falcon. 2. Falcons. 3. Birds—Protection] I. Hewett, Richard R., ill. II. Title.
QL696.F34A76   1985   598'.918   84-15576
    ISBN 0-87614-225-0 (lib. bdg.)
    ISBN 0-87614-523-3 (pbk.)

Manufactured in the United States of America

6 7 8 9 10 11 – P/JR – 00 99 98 97 96 95

We would like to thank many people for their generous contributions of time and expertise and for their cheerful cooperation with us while we were working on this book. In particular we are grateful to Brian Walton (pictured above), head of the Santa Cruz Predatory Bird Research Group located at the University of California Santa Cruz, and to members of his staff including Gail Naylor and Merlyn Felton; to Jim Jennings and Sam Sumida of the Western Foundation of Vertebrate Zoology; to Mark Robertson; and to The Peregrine Fund, whose concern over the survival of the peregrine falcon has helped prevent the extinction of this beautiful and remarkable bird.

High above a tall bank building in downtown Los Angeles, a peregrine falcon soars in the air looking for food below. The peregrine falcon is a wild bird that we do not normally think of as a city dweller. Yet the peregrine is at home among the high-rise buildings, which in many ways are like the cliffs and mountains where peregrines usually live. Window and roof ledges make good places to perch and to lay eggs, and the streets below are filled with pigeons, starlings, sparrows, and other small birds that peregrines like to eat. Today more and more peregrines are becoming part of city life as part of a special program to try to save this beautiful and powerful bird from **extinction**.

For centuries the peregrine was prized by kings and falconers who used it to hunt. Bird lovers too have always admired the peregrine. Yet a few years ago it was feared that soon there would be no more peregrines. Man's pollution of the environment with the poison DDT had interfered with the birds' ability to produce babies. The total number of peregrines was growing smaller each year. In 1970 there were only two known pairs of nesting peregrines in California. Until the 1940s, when DDT began to be used, there had been nearly two hundred. In the eastern United States the peregrine had already become extinct by 1970. Only with man's help could the peregrine be saved.

Peregrine falcons are found all over the world. The scientific name for those found in the United States is *Falco peregrinus anatum*. Other falcons living in the United States are the **gyrfalcon**, the **prairie falcon**, the **merlin**, and the **kestrel**. Although the numbers of these other falcons have been reduced by man, none of them is endangered like the peregrine.

Falcons are similar in many ways to birds in the hawk family. When flying, however, a falcon has pointed wings, which are better suited to speed, whereas a hawk has wide-spread wing feathers, which are better suited to soaring.

You can recognize an adult peregrine because it appears to wear a large black moustache. Both males and females have the same color markings but, as with all hawks and falcons, the female is larger and stronger than the male. A female peregrine is usually about twenty inches (50 cm) long and weighs about thirty ounces (840 g). A male is about fifteen inches (37.5 cm) long and weighs about eighteen ounces (504 g). The male is sometimes called a **tiercel** from the French word meaning "third" because he is about a third smaller than the female peregrine.

Falcons, like hawks, eagles, and owls, catch and eat other animals. They are **predators**. The peregrine specializes in a diet of birds. In the United States, peregrines used to be called duck hawks because they were seen around marshes and occasionally hunted ducks.

8

The peregrine's body, like those of other predatory birds, is well adapted for hunting. Its strong feet and sharp talons are ideal for catching and carrying, and its beak is designed for tearing. The peregrine's eyesight is so keen that it has been compared to a person being able to read a newspaper a mile away! A soaring peregrine can see a bird hundreds of feet below.

After spotting a bird, the peregrine points its head down, tucks in its wings and feet, and transforms its body into the shape of a speeding bullet. As it begins to dive, it pumps its wings to increase its speed up to 200 miles per hour! No bird alive is faster than a diving peregrine. When the peregrine reaches its prey, it grabs it with its feet, then quickly kills it by breaking its neck. The peregrine then either carries the dead bird to a protected place and eats it, or brings it back to the nest to feed hungry babies.

Baby peregrines are usually called chicks, although a chick in a wild nest is also called an **eyas**. Unfortunately for most peregrines in the United States, there have been fewer and fewer hungry chicks in wild nests to feed.

Most of the smaller birds that peregrines in the United States eat spend the winter in Central and South America. There they eat grains and insects that have been sprayed with DDT. DDT is a poison used by farmers to kill insects that are harmful to crops. When the birds eat food with DDT on it, the poison is stored in their bodies. Later, when the peregrines eat these birds, they eat the poison too. The more birds the peregrines eat, the more DDT they store.

Scientists have found that DDT causes birds to lay eggs with shells that are too thin. When they measure the shells of hatched or broken eggs, they find that the thinnest shells are those with the most DDT in them. When parent birds sit on these eggs to keep them warm, the thin shells often break. Thin-shelled eggs also lose moisture faster than thick-shelled eggs. Often the chick growing inside the egg dies because the egg dries out too much. By helping the eggs with thin shells to hatch, scientists can combat some of the effects of DDT.

Most wild peregrines nest on high ledges on rocky cliffs. These nest sites are called **eyries**. A pair of peregrines makes a nest in an eyrie by scraping clean a small area in the stones or sand. In the scrape the female usually lays three eggs. Scientists carefully watch each peregrine nest. Then if they feel that the eggs are unlikely to hatch without help, they borrow them for a while, but first they let the birds sit on the eggs for five days. This seems to improve the eggs' chances of hatching in the laboratory.

Because the cliffs where peregrines nest are so steep, only a mountain climber can reach a nest. When he approaches the nest, the angry parents screech and swoop at him. The mountain climber quickly and carefully puts each speckled egg into a padded box. He then replaces the eggs he has taken with plaster eggs which look just like real peregrine eggs. These fake eggs will fool the parent birds. After the mountain climber leaves, the parents will return to the nest and sit on the plaster eggs as if they were their own.

It is important to keep the parent birds interested in the nest. After the eggs have hatched, the mountain climber will bring the babies back so that the parents can take care of them.

When the mountain climber gets back to the top of the cliff, he puts the eggs into a portable **incubator**. The incubator will keep them safe and warm on their ride back to the laboratory.

Three places in the United States where peregrine eggs are hatched are in Ithaca (New York), Boise (Idaho), and Santa Cruz (California). Brian Walton and the staff of the Santa Cruz Predatory Bird Research Group (SCPBRG) collect eggs and release birds throughout the western United States. The laboratory at the SCPBRG center is used for hatching eggs and caring for the newly hatched peregrine chicks.

In the laboratory each egg is carefully weighed. Then it is held in front of a bright light in a dark room. This is called **candling**. When an egg is candled, the shadow of the chick growing inside and a lighter area at the large end of the egg can be seen. The lighter area is called the air pocket.

Then the egg is placed on a rack inside an incubator. The incubator keeps the egg warm and moist. Each day the egg will be weighed and candled again. As the chick grows, water slowly evaporates from the egg, making room for the air pocket to get bigger. The egg's weight shows how much water it is losing. If it is losing water too quickly, the incubator can be made more moist.

Wild birds turn their eggs constantly as they move around in the nest. But in the laboratory, people must carefully turn each egg four or five times each day. This prevents the growing chick from sticking to the inside of the eggshell. If the eggs are not turned, they will not hatch.

Sometimes eggs are found with shells so thin that they have already begun to crack. Then people in the laboratory try to repair them with glue. Sometimes eggs are also waxed to prevent them from losing moisture. Everything possible is done to make sure that each egg hatches into a healthy peregrine chick.

The eggs are kept in the incubator until they are 31½ days old. Then they are carefully watched for the first signs of hatching.

Each chick has a hard pointed knob on the top of its beak. This is called an **egg tooth.** The chick pushes against the inside of the shell with its egg tooth and breaks the shell.

The first crack in the egg is called the **pip.** When the pip appears, the egg is moved to a special hatching chamber. There the egg will take 24 to 48 hours to hatch. During this time somebody watches it all the time. Some chicks are too weak to break out of their shells. Then the scientists are there to help them.

Often two eggs begin to hatch at about the same time. Then they are put next to each other in the hatcher. When a chick is ready to hatch, it begins

to peep inside its shell. The two chicks can hear each other peep. This seems to encourage them to move around and break their shells. Sometimes when there is only one egg, the scientists make peeping sounds for the chick to hear.

Starting at the pip, the chick slowly turns, pressing its egg tooth against the shell. Soon the crack becomes a ring around the shell. Then the chick pushes its head against the top of the shell, and the shell pops open. After hatching, the egg tooth is no longer needed, and in a week or so it falls off.

The newly hatched chick is wet and its down feathers are matted together. A cotton swab is used to clean the feathers. If necessary, ointment is put on the chick's navel to prevent infection. In the shell the chick gets nutrients from the yolk through its navel. Normally, by the time a chick hatches, the yolk has been totally absorbed and the navel has closed.

In the wild, a mother bird **broods** her chicks by sitting on top of them to keep them warm and dry. In the laboratory, the dry chick is placed with one or more others in a small container called a **brooder**. A heater keeps the chicks warm. The chick will rest in the brooder for eight to twelve hours. Then it will be ready for its first meal.

In the wild the father peregrine hunts birds and brings them back to the nest. Then he and the mother peregrine tear off small bits of meat to feed each chick. The hungry chicks beg for food by peeping and opening their mouths wide.

Bird meat is also used to feed chicks in the laboratory. Usually the chicks are fed quail, although adult birds are also fed pigeon and chicken meat. First the meat is put through a meat grinder to break it into small pieces. The newly hatched chicks are then fed tiny pieces with tweezers. For somewhat older chicks the ground meat can be squeezed through a bag with a nozzle.

Like many birds, falcons have pouches in their necks to store food. These are called **crops**. Food first goes to the crop and then to the stomach. A bird feeder knows that a chick has had enough when the crop begins to bulge.

During the day, young peregrine chicks need to be fed every three to five hours. At night they sleep eight hours between feedings.

Even though the peregrine chicks are cared for by people, it is important that they remain wild. During the first week or so, the chicks cannot see very well. Then it does not matter if people feed them directly. But as they get older, their contact with people must be limited.

Young animals identify with the other animals they see during the first weeks of life. This is called **imprinting**. Most young animals only see their parents in early life, and they imprint on them.

Peregrines raised in the laboratory that will be returned to the wild must be imprinted on adult peregrines. One way to help them do this is to feed them with a peregrine-shaped puppet. The puppet fools the peregrine chicks and they behave as if it were a real bird.

When a peregrine chick is three days to a week old, it is put into the nest of an adult bird that has been imprinted on people. At the SCPBRG center, adult birds are kept in barnlike buildings. Each large, open-air room in these buildings has bars across the top to let in air and light. Each room also has perches and nesting ledges for the birds.

Unfortunately there are not enough adult peregrines at the center to care for all the hatched chicks. Another more common bird, the prairie falcon, is very much like the peregrine, and it is

often used as a substitute parent for very young peregrine chicks. During the breeding season, a female prairie falcon will care for adopted peregrine chicks. She will keep them warm and feed them as if they were her own. When the chicks are one to two weeks old, they are put into nests of peregrines which are not imprinted on people. Then, at the age of three weeks, the young peregrines are ready to go back to wild nests.

Before a bird goes back to the wild, a metal band is put on its leg. The band identifies the bird and helps people keep track of it as it grows up.

Then the chicks are put into a special wooden pack and taken to the nest site. There the mountain climber puts the pack on his back and climbs to the nest. He removes the plaster eggs and puts in the young chicks. Then he leaves as quickly as possible. He does not want to disturb the parent birds any more than necessary.

The parent birds soon return to the nest. Although they are surprised at first to find healthy chicks instead of eggs in their nest, the parents quickly accept their new babies. The hungry chicks beg for food, and the parents' natural response is to feed them. The chicks are on their way to growing up as wild peregrines.

Most wild birds do not breed well in captivity. They are easily disturbed by people and by loud noises. The cages at the SCPBRG center are made so that the birds rarely see people, although people can see the birds through tiny peepholes.

In the bird buildings a radio is constantly played. The sound blocks out most noises from outside. The radio also helps the birds become used to people's voices. Then they are less likely to be startled when people make noises outside their chambers.

Pairs of peregrine falcons at the SCPBRG center build nests and breed just as birds do in the wild. Their chicks can be released to help increase the number of wild peregrines.

Both in the wild and in captivity, peregrines normally raise only one nest of chicks each year. If the eggs are destroyed, however, the birds will lay a second set. In the wild, peregrine eggs might be eaten by other birds or animals. At the center, scientists purposely take away the first eggs from each pair of breeding falcons and hatch them in an incubator. The birds then lay another set of eggs. In this way each pair of birds can produce twice as many chicks as usual.

During its six weeks in the nest, a peregrine grows from a fluffy chick covered with soft down to a fully feathered bird the size of its parents. These first juvenile feathers are a mottled brown color. The peregrine will get its adult feathers at the beginning of its second year.

Three-week-old peregrine chicks are put into known wild nests that have parent birds on them when possible, but because there are so few peregrines left in the wild, soon all the wild peregrine nests are filled. Some peregrine chicks are put into wild prairie falcon nests. Others are released on their own when they are old enough to fly.

In the wild, a young peregrine is ready to fly at the age of six weeks. Then it leaves the nest and tries to hunt for food. At first it is not a very good hunter. Its parents will help it and continue to feed it. When juvenile peregrines from the laboratory are put into the wild, they have no parents to help them. Then people must help them instead.

Usually the birds are released near cliff tops or mountain ledges far away from where people live. They are placed in a box at the release site when they are about five weeks old. Sometimes the box must be carried to the release site by a helicopter.

The box has bars across one side, but the people involved try to stay out of the birds' sight. From behind, they drop

meat into the box for the birds. Then after a week, the box is opened and the birds are allowed to fly free.

People stay at the site and put food out each day until the birds learn to take care of themselves. This may take four to five weeks. When the birds no longer need to return to the release site for food, the people's job is finished.

In addition to its identification band, each bird also wears a small radio transmitter. The radio makes beeping sounds which can be heard with a radio receiver. During the first few weeks on its own, a bird sometimes gets lost or in trouble. Then people can find it by tracking the beeps over the radio receiver. After a few weeks the transmitter will no longer be needed, and it will fall off the bird.

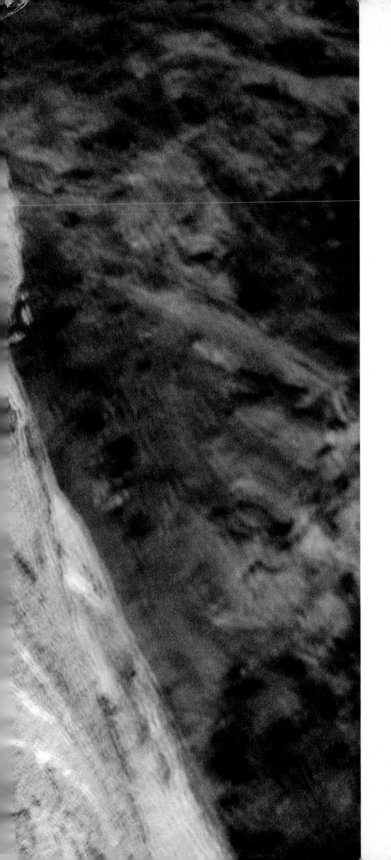

Most birds are set free in wild places where peregrines once lived but are now gone. It is hoped that the new peregrines will stay there, build nests, and bring up chicks of their own.

Some peregrines are released in cities, and they seem to adapt well to city life. Los Angeles, New York, Washington, Baltimore, Edmonton, London, and Nairobi are just some of the cities around the world where peregrines live. Some live on the ledges of office buildings. Others have built nests on tall bridges. In England peregrines lived for many years in the spire of Salisbury Cathedral.

In cities peregrines are usually released from the tops of tall buildings. As in the wild, people stay and feed the birds until they can take care of themselves. After a pair of peregrines has claimed a building ledge as a nest site, scientists sometimes build a nest there for the birds. They may even put a fake egg into the nest. They hope that this will encourage the birds to begin laying their own eggs.

Peregrines usually do not mate and have young until their third year. In their first breeding years in the wild, peregrines can raise their own chicks. But as the birds get older and store more and more DDT in their bodies, their egg shells will become dangerously thin. As long as people use DDT as an insecticide, peregrines will be endangered and will continue to need man's help to survive.

Peregrines must survive many dangers before they are old enough to produce their own chicks. Many hurt themselves when they collide with man-made objects such as fences or telephone and electric wires. Others are shot by unthinking people. Centers like the SCPBRG help sick and wounded peregrines. Endangered birds like peregrines need all the help they can get.

The peregrine falcon is a beautiful bird, and it would be sad to let it become extinct simply through ignorance or carelessness. Many animals that once roamed the earth are now gone because man destroyed or polluted their environments. For the present, the peregrine falcon has been saved from extinction. Through the work of many people around the world its numbers are increasing each year. If you are lucky, maybe where you live, you can see one of these magnificent birds soaring high in the sky.

Glossary

brood: When parent birds sit on their eggs or chicks to keep them warm, they are brooding.

brooder: a small, heated container designed to keep chicks warm

candling: holding an egg in front of a bright light in order to see the chick growing inside

crop: a pouch for storing food located in the necks of some birds

egg tooth: the hard, pointed knob on top of a young chick's beak, used for breaking out of the egg

extinction: When all the animals of a certain kind, or species, have died, that species is extinct.

eyas: the name for a falcon chick in a wild nest

eyrie: the nest site of a wild peregrine, usually located on a high ledge of a rocky cliff

gyrfalcon: the largest type of falcon. Gyrfalcons can be two feet (60 cm) or more in length.

imprinting: the identification a baby animal makes during the first few weeks of its life with the other animals around it, usually its parents

incubator: a warm, moist case used to hatch eggs

kestrel: the smallest falcon found in America

merlin: a falcon very similar to the peregrine in color but smaller in size

pip: the first crack a hatching chick makes in the egg

prairie falcon: a falcon that resembles a peregrine but has lighter markings. Prairie falcons live in the western United States.

predator: an animal that kills and eats other animals. Falcons are predators.

tiercel: a male falcon